MW00489243

Found.
Still lost.

healing through reflection

Poetry by
Ashley Nichole Walkowiak
and John M. Nester

Photographs by
Ashley Nichole Walkowiak

BROWN POSEY PRESS

an imprint of Sunbury Press, Inc.
Mechanicsburg, PA USA

an imprint of Sunbury Press, Inc.
Mechanicsburg, PA USA

Copyright © 2022 by Ashley Nichole Walkowiak and John M. Nester.
Cover Copyright © 2022 by Sunbury Press, Inc.

Sunbury Press supports copyright. Copyright fuels creativity, encourages diverse voices, promotes free speech, and creates a vibrant culture. Thank you for buying an authorized edition of this book and for complying with copyright laws. Except for the quotation of short passages for the purpose of criticism and review, no part of this publication may be reproduced, scanned, or distributed in any form without permission. You are supporting writers and allowing Sunbury Press to continue to publish books for every reader. For information contact Sunbury Press, Inc., Subsidiary Rights Dept., PO Box 548, Boiling Springs, PA 17007 USA or legal@sunburypress.com.

For information about special discounts for bulk purchases, please contact Sunbury Press Orders Dept. at (855) 338-8359 or orders@sunburypress.com.

To request one of our authors for speaking engagements or book signings, please contact Sunbury Press Publicity Dept. at publicity@sunburypress.com.

FIRST BROWN POSEY PRESS EDITION: February 2022

Set in Adobe Garamond Pro | Interior design by Crystal Devine | Cover design by Ashley Nichole Walkowiak | Photographs by Ashley Nichole Walkowiak | Edited by Jennifer Cappello.

Publisher's Cataloging-in-Publication Data
Names: Walkowiak, Ashley Nichole, author | Nester, John M., author.
Title: Found. Still lost. / Ashley Nichole Walkowiak and John M. Nester.
Description: First trade paperback edition. | Mechanicsburg, PA : Brown Posey Press, 2022.
Summary: *Found. Still lost.* is an empowering collection of poetry and images exploring the depths of trauma and inviting us all to heal through the validation of our innermost feelings. One of the best ways to combat the immediate and long-term effects of trauma is to remind ourselves that our emotions are the mind's healthy ways of coping with extraordinary events. Within these pages, you will see a reflection of the human condition and be invited to begin your healing journey from the present moment.
Identifiers: ISBN : 978-1-62006-905-9 (trade paperback).
Subjects: POETRY / American / General | PHOTOGRAPHY / Individual Photographers / Artists' Books | BODY, MIND & SPIRIT / Healing / General | SELF-HELP/ Post-Traumatic Stress Disorder (PTSD).

Product of the United States of America
0 1 1 2 3 5 8 13 21 34 55

Continue the Enlightenment!

Contents

Introduction

Before beginning, it is important to note that this may be a difficult read.

This book is dedicated to every soul who has struggled with loss. Be that the permanent loss of a loved one, or the deepest moment of loss of self. You are not alone.

Trauma, sparked by loss, violation, struggles of the human condition, can leave us juggling feelings of shock, confusion, denial, and grief. Experiencing trauma can manifest physical conditions such as anxiety, panic, headaches, dizziness, poor concentration, and flashbacks. Feelings of detachment, isolation from family and friends, and struggling to complete typical daily tasks are all common responses to trauma.

One of the best ways to combat these effects is to remind ourselves that our emotions are the mind's healthy ways of coping with extraordinary events. Seeing and hearing the uncomfortable thoughts and feelings reflected in these pages is meant to remind us all that processing loss and trauma is what our bodies need to do to heal and move forward.

You are not alone. Even as the trauma you've experienced has shaped you, the joyful moments will shape you as well.

If you or someone you know is struggling with depression, PTSD, or suicidal ideation, free and confidential help is available through Lifeline at 1-800-273-8255.

Allow Us to Introduce Ourselves

by John

These are the words you whisper
When you look out the window
The secrets you speak to nobody
These are the sounds you scream
At the deaf bus driver
These are your mistakes
The siren call of a thousand wasted days
Another skeleton left
At your friend's grave
These are the lost riddles
From your grandfather's Alzheimer's
The things we're too afraid to tell
To an audience
The ones that only your cat knows
The thoughts that we so often
Ignore ourselves
There is truth
Behind the mirror
You just have to
Turn on the light

Strands of Silence
by John

> We carefully select
> strands of silence
> Braiding them into blankets
> of bitterness
> Wrapping ourselves in the warmth
> of resentment
> The truth is
> I'm more alone now
> Than I've ever been
> And it doesn't matter
> How I kick and scream

You're leagues away
You slip on empty bottles
Broken glass sticking
To the gum on your sole
Your shadow is my closet
Our reflections
Caress each other in the mirror
But our flesh never touches
And no words are spoken
Surrounded by silence

If These Walls Could Speak

by John

Speak about the wall
The one you tried to climb
The one with no footholds
That seemed limitless
And when you asked
They ran off
Instead of kneeling down
And cupping their hands
So you laid back
Alone
Head against the stone and mortar
Discerning shapes from clouds
Noticing the way they quivered
With every blow of head on stone
Trying to remember
What the sun felt like on your skin
Before it hid behind the wall
Grass withering
Turning hard and brown
Beneath your feet
Tell us how you waited for the wall
To topple
Waited for age to take its toll
And when it finally fell
Crushing you beneath its weight
For a moment you saw the sun again
Dazzling in its beauty

Note to Self

by Ashley

When I lay me down
And my eyes are heavy and tired
I know it's because
They have not looked into yours

For all of the climbing
When I break the top
And it's dark instead of light
I know that if I just reach out
Your illumination
Will break the night

Decorations

by John

Withdrawn from society
Downtime is a poison
For a drowned mind
Needling my way through
The dirt and cobwebs
The mainline was
Just wasted time
I break my spine
To reach for
The colored paper
Beneath the veins
Of the pine tree
Rope from the branch
To my arm
Or my neck
We'll just be
Decorations
Existing beneath the stars
And angels
I held my chest
But I gave my last breath
In and out
In
And
Out

An Outlier

by John

She watched the tree all spring
An outlier.
It shot toward the heavens
Reaching higher than the rest
A wisp of brown and green
Towering over the burdened.
It gave her
A sense of peace
Like she was
Being watched over.
Until that day in mid-summer
When it cracked.
Maybe it was the weight
Of such lofty expectations.
Maybe it was one gust too many.
But it leaned there
Precariously
Two hundred feet in the air.

She watched that trunk all autumn
An outlier.
It leaned toward the earth
A weight perched.
Waiting for an unsuspecting victim
But none walked beneath it
It crashed harmlessly
And she looked up
Just in time to see.
It forced a path
To the ground
Then landed with an
unexpected grace.

She breathlessly walked over
Ripped off a lifeless branch
From the uppermost portion
Looking it over
Examining this piece
That she watched
Through four seasons
Casually
She snapped it over her knee
And tossed it into the fire
Letting it burn
Into the others
That it once
Towered over.

Lost-latitude

by John

The truth is that
I'm sorry you don't know
How many battles
I've fought, even recently
The ones I know can't be won
How many empty stamped envelopes
We've self-addressed
And sent to nowhere
Always surprised
When it's our own veins
Waving goodbye
From inside the chemical package
The way I chew the dirt
From around the coffin
Shitting out splinters and resolve
How many times
I've cracked my spine
Holding back mudslides and tsunamis
So you don't have to
Tread water with me
And I wave from the middle of it
Reassurance that
I'm out for a quick dip
That there is nothing to worry about
And I'm sorry
That I didn't let you see
The smile slide down my face
And slip around my neck
You were right there
I just couldn't get the dirt
Out of my throat

Twisting Above Me

by John

She told me how she grew
From the ashes of a charred life
How she spun a negative into a positive
And grabbed just enough light
To keep going

And sure
Her form was a bit twisted
She paints
With contrasting colors
And writes pictures
Things that don't always
Belong together
Like self and love

She tells me that
I need to learn
To see the beauty
In the pain
And if I hate
Being cooped up
That I need to learn
To dance in the rain

She extends her branches
Up not out
Learning at a young age
That you have to
Let people reach
For a helping hand

All she wants is a little peace
After being made to run
Before she knew
How to stand

So I try
To put my lower level
Income bracket skills
To good use
Tearing off shingles
And knocking down walls
Knowing that
Even if it kills me
She'll finally be able to
Stretch herself out

Phosphenes Days

by Ashley

I'm a half-dead kinda girl
Half a waltz
Half a smile
Half a line

You half-killed me
When you killed you

And what doesn't kill us
Only makes us half

Flowering Cocoon

by John

She loved me
She loved me not
I ignored the foreboding knocks in my stomach
Until they crawled out of my mouth
And landed in a puddle on the floor
She loved me in knots
Tangled up in a mirage of what love
Is supposed to be
Until the threads engulfed me
A repulsive cocoon
More than just a loose thread
She loathes me
I am a reminder of what she can't be
Free and poor or rich and enslaved
We're neither
Shackled and broken
To this world and each other
She loves me
Watching me rot

| Found. Still lost.

Pirouettes

by Ashley

No words would come
When I saw you there
Only a private gift
The fairest dance
Of highest rite
I solely offer
My eyes collapsed
Before my knees
You will come back
If only I dance
I know you will
Please

I would have sworn
My burning tears
Could've melted away
Your distorted face
Make all once clear
For they warmed my cheeks
But not our embrace
The only thing
Left to say
Was not goodbye
No, not for us
Only pirouettes
In our reveries

Surroundings

by John

I'm still learning
Through all the dark days
Where the only sound
Was the blood rushing through my ears
Through the drives to nowhere
Anywhere that could get me as far
Away from me
As possible
The drinks, the drugs
The girls, the stillness
The motion, the sleep
The sobriety
The mirrors

The mirrors I'm still staring into
All these years later
I lay down in the broken glass
Hoping I can see truth
When I sleep
I'm still learning
But dreams speak in riddles
Even if your own face
Is staring back at you
The lines are too blurred
And the depth is too much to discern
The surroundings blend into the
Reflection
And I can't tell me apart

Median
by Ashley

I can't give you an answer
If the question won't come out

And I can't rid these demons
If your eyes are full of doubt

Deft Perception

by Ashley

I've got a pocketful of reasons
Why I'm here behind your door
Not wearing them for you to see
That crumpled cotton on the floor
Can join the monsters 'neath your bed sheets
But pull me close and lie so sweet
Tell me the light will never catch us
And you will never flee
Leave no doubt within these shadows
Join me now inside the hollows
Empty pockets
Broken stars
And all that glows
Begins with sorrow

| Found. Still lost.

Lost and Found Courtyard

by John

Her face was stoic the last time he saw it
As still as the mountains he now chases
Jaw set and just the faintest glimmer in her eye
She turned and walked away before he did
He watched her dress waft in the wind as she walked to the swing
A final, irresolute wave goodbye
But that face isn't what he remembers now
No, the face in his mind is smiling
Sunlight reflecting off her face, pure
He remembers the graveyard, their graveyard
That was more than 2,000 miles ago
The lines on the road blur together
Forcing him to snap back into time, live in the now
But her face is still dancing between the lines
The only sound in his ears is the steady
Raaahrbum, raaahrbum, raaahrbum of the tires on the road
The music stopped five towns ago
So he drives on, silently, seeing her face in the mirrors
And on the pavement
Running from it and toward it at the same time
"Don't stop for a drink,
You can get through this"
"Just a few more hundred miles"
"Faster, faster, farther, farther"
The road is black, as the desert around it
Illuminated solely by the numerous stars in the sky
"How will I know
When I get there?"

Here Lies

by John

With enough plots to bury the bodies of her past
They're history.
But it's hers.
Some people,
Like trees,
Don't carry dead weight well.
And in order to grow
They need to be pruned.
Sometimes hard,
Neglecting what gets cut off.
Discarded or turned into compost,
Buried beneath a willow with a simple
Handwritten picket
Stuck in the dirt.
"Here lies the husband who once struck me"
"The relatives who never wrote to me"
"The sister who wouldn't be bothered
To testify on my behalf."
Here lies
A simple misspelling.
Or a subconscious attempt
At confronting her compulsive need
To destroy.

Momentary Vagary

by Ashley

I only see your face
When the lightning flashes
Searching the bruise-colored clouds
The clap restores my heartbeat
And I dance in the flooded skies
I dance in you

And for a moment

I'm alive again

When I was Jung

by John

I am Frankenstein
I am Frankenstein's monster
Give me my father's addictions
And my mother's selfishness
Give me Chuck's discontentment
Jack's mania
Michael's ideas
I can be more
Than what I've created
What you've created
Strive for Beauty's joy
And my father's hope
My mother's love
My dog's loyalty
I am Frankenstein's
Sense of desperation
I am a man playing God
I've created life
Watch me destroy it

Nevermore . . . and

by John

Hop off the carousel
It's time to grow
I know you won't tell
The difference between
The lions and tigers
And barefaced angel
That you thought was permanently
Stitched to my face
Wrap itself around my neck
And choke out the childhood
How many grimaces does it take
To fill a glass
Drink it down
A teaspoon of sugar
Thoughts will drown
Broken rosaries
Can't pull the fairy tales
From the pit of adulthood
Even Rapunzel
Went back up
To her tower

Original Muse

by John

I had shouted my warnings

    Into the wind
Carried away to deaf ears
Life with me
Would morph into death
I was addicted
To struggle

Pain was my original muse
And it still has me
Wrapped around its finger
Or bicep
But she insisted
That she loved me
And she could deal
With my demons
Even if I lusted after them

But now
I can feel her slipping
She tires of being broken
Left with the misfit toys
While I chase a dream
And she's tired
Of me
Running toward solitude

But if you can't follow me
Into the darkness
That builds itself
Around my vision
Can you leave me a rope
So I can climb my way back
To you

Scratching at the Decomposition

by John

I relish the way my flesh sneers at me
When it's incomplete, a seam
An everlasting smirk, toothless
That grins up at me
As I squeeze and pinch it together
We're nothing but sacks of meat
Bags of blood and bone
Organic material
Waiting to decompose
And that's the joke
The godless prank
We're all rot
Our substance becoming the grass
And the trees
So we kill ourselves again

A species-specific suicide
And all of our love
And art
And contributions
Are forgotten
Decay feeding the trees
That become our homes
And the oil that fuels our cars
Burning our own memories
Becoming smoke

Miss Steps

by John

Slate worn on a necklace
Pretend it was a jewel
Dependent on your shadows
Still discerning all your truths
Addicted to the music
That your organs make
Hearts ran off the same circuit
Too many volts create pain
Your brain exists in waves
Magnetic in their complexity
Hormones lapping up the sweat
I roll over while you're exiting
I'll pretend we predicted
These pretenses and missteps
If pain is pleasure
Then we were perfection
Where do I go next?
Sweet slippers on the steps
Of my mind's short mishap
Please don't tap upon the glass
I'll go backward if you like
Don't push me forward too fast
Two left feet
Hard to do right
It takes me three times longer
Following the signs
And your fireflies
In the night

Identity Crisis

by John

Identity crisis, break glass to see the light
Rub together two panes
Drown out the darkness
Polish your thumb on your
Forefinger
It's the thought that counts
But not quite high enough
You arrived at a fork
And I watched as you
Deliberated before
Barreling through the center
Creating your own path
Apart from all three
Praying to the stars
Waiting for the sun to light the way
But glass can't be fixed
It needs to be replaced
And with no money
No hope and no reflection
You're still chasing
Your heaven
Just start asking
The right questions

DandyLion Queen

by Ashley

She collects wishes
Never promises
And blows them
On the wind

This one is intricate
One is uncharted
One for a whisper
And the smell of rain

She wishes not for passion
Not for vindication either
She wishes for the promise
Of a day disillusioned

Secrets

by John

She said
"What makes you,
You?"
His only reply was
"Secrets"
What he didn't say was
"It's a secret"
He said
"Secrets"
And that was
In itself, a secret
Because what he meant was
What makes me, me
Is keeping secrets
My won secrets
The mysteries of an ominous past
The dreams of a bright future
The memories that haunt his nights
Other people's secrets
Where she was when her husband
Thought she was visiting
Her sick aunt
What he
And his secretary do
On their lunch breaks
What she has recurring nightmares
About
He said,
"What makes me, me
Is secrets"

Unseen

by John

That familiar feeling
Watching your toes dangle off the cliff
Seeing the breeze blow your cigarette when it falls
From your cracked lips
Wondering if it will treat your body the same way
Rest is too much to ask of life
No rest for the weary
And no tissues for the teary
We force our way onward
Walking into the sun
Waiting for the ground to be pulled
From beneath our feet
But every time I expect to fall
When I take those steps out past the edge
I hover
Held up by unseen hands
How does the same air that fills my lungs
Become hands under my arms
Keeping me on unsteady feet

Mellifluous Man

by Ashley

In the waiting room of my life

You were just the magazine I paged through

But how scenic our days

How worn our pages

How hollow our words

Sermons of the Solitary

by John

Tell them why you air out your dirty laundry
Why you leave your tear-stained pillowcases
And bloody towels waving in the wind
Night terrors and wet dreams
Daring the neighbors to judge you or ask questions
I can't tell you all my secrets
Because I'm still looking for them myself
But I can let you watch the process
While you dig graves with grenades
Hoping to bury who you don't want to be
And maybe find the occasional bauble

You can't discern the differences in the soil
But you know you're getting close
When you see your old Spider-Man hat
Or a box of notes neatly folded in a thousand paper footballs
The ink blots and the decades-old cigarette butts
The dried-out husks of the hearts that you stole and hid
You know you're getting close when you see the broken mirror
And start to forget who is staring at you

Somnambulist

by Ashley

As I walk through the valley
Your shadow is the veil

Backward through the battlefield
Of enlightened suggestion

A sacrifice, perfected poetry
You return with tortured crown

Asking not for what I know
Give me what I understand

Woven into this obsession
Feed the night your silver leaves

Conflagrantly
These indiscretions

About the Artists

Siblings Ashley and John were raised with an appreciation for literature and language. When John enrolled in a creative writing class and asked Ashley for some of her photographs to draw inspiration from, the two realized they loved working together.

This second edition comes after the loss of their sister, Aereyelle, and brings an intrinsic understanding of the depths of grief.

ASHLEY NICHOLE WALKOWIAK began studying film and darkroom photography at the age of thirteen. After a sexual assault left her riddled with PTSD, she put down her camera but never lost her passion for the arts. Believing that the purpose of art is understanding and connection, Ashley later continued to write and photograph life while working with a trauma therapist on her healing journey.

portrait by Chad Harnish

Now a wife and mother of three, she works for the Pennsylvania Office of Victim Advocate, where she amplifies the voice of crime victims and works to cultivate societal change that will lessen violence in our communities.

JOHN MICHAEL NESTER is a business owner, mentor, and an adoring husband and father of three who hates his portrait being taken. He is an avid writer, using words to identify the depths of the human condition. His raw composition rips open the scabs of men living the American life, torn between the energy needed to provide for their families and the energy needed to dissect and heal their own cultural and generational wounds.

Both John and Ashley live in Central Pennsylvania, where they continue to drive their loving parents just a wee bit insane, even in adulthood.

Made in the USA
Monee, IL
18 February 2022

91429330R00037